MW01491610

Leading Through Loss

NAVIGATING LOSS & MANIFESTING WINS

BUDDLEWRITER

LEADING THROUGH LOSS: Navigating Loss and Manifesting Wins

Copyright © 2023 by Priscilla Mendez

All rights reserved. Except as permitted under the U.S. Copyright Act of 1976, no part of this publication may be reproduced, distributed, or transmitted in any form or by any means or stored in a database or retrieval system without the prior written permission of the publisher/ author.

This book is a work of the author's experiences and personal perspective. However, it is sold with the understanding that the author and publisher are not engaged in rendering professional psychological advice. The author and publisher expressly disclaim any liability incurred from the use or application of the contents of this book.

For permission, special orders, corporate sales, etc., don't hesitate to get in touch with the author at priscillamendez65@gmail.com or the publisher at info@buddlewriter.com

MENDEZ, PRISCILLA
LEADING THROUGH LOSS: Navigating Loss and Manifesting Wins

ISBN: 978-1-932448-50-4 (paperback) Available in eBook

1. Self Help 2. Marriage 3. Self-Development 4. Professional
Printed and bound in the United States of America

Published By:
BUDDLEWRITER ®
www.buddlewriter.com

PRISCILLA MENDEZ

Leading Through Loss

NAVIGATING LOSS & MANIFESTING WINS

BUDDLEWRITER

Dedication

This book is dedicated to the three remarkable human beings I call my Little Family!

You have kept me afloat with your love, belief in me, and resilience during a heartbreaking time for us.

MOM, you are the strongest woman I know. In turn, you made a strong woman out of me. You made something out of nothing with your unconditional love; for that, I am forever grateful. You've shared my suffering, accomplishments, setbacks, and everything in between. Your eyes have cried the same tears as mine; only a mother could do that without hesitation or question. I am eternally grateful that you are mine.

JUSTIN, you are and will always be my first love. I realize that, being a young mom, I didn't always get things right. But loving you with the very depths of my soul is something for which I'll always be proud. I love our new season, our understanding of one another, and us growing in sync with each other! I shall live the rest of my days trying to make things right - you sacrificed so much, and I am so grateful for your love and protection!

LEILANI, you remain the most selfless person I know. You overheard something I was ashamed of for so long, yet, you, my little gem, took a devastating situation and helped paint a beautiful picture from a positive perspective. Your smile, love, and laughter have reminded me that our bright future is worth fighting for. You understand so much about life, love, and me as a woman, mom, and educator. I can't thank you enough for authentically embracing my change and being my biggest cheerleader.

May this book be a testament to the power of love, family, and resilience; may it inspire others to navigate loss and manifest wins in their lives.

Love always,

Table of Contents

With Self-Empowerment Worksheets &

Activities

Introduction

Have you ever encountered someone who seems to have everything figured out? Someone who radiates positivity and success with a fulfilling career, financial stability, and an almost 'perfect family'? That was me - the epitome of poise, grace, and ambition. I found success in unexpected places and used my wit and charm to connect with those around me. Life appeared perfect, and I was content living in my perfectly packaged world until an unexpected turn of events knocked me off my feet (quite literally).

During the COVID-19 pandemic, life as I knew it changed in a way I could have never anticipated. Who knew that the pandemic would change the course of the profession I had dedicated myself to for the last 20 years? Who knew the words *"I want a divorce"* would tear my heart apart and lead me down a dark path I never knew existed?

This book is my story, my truth, and frankly, a coping mechanism to deal with personal loss. It was written as a tool for healing and helping others going through similar experiences.

Since the onset of COVID, I have worked alongside incredible educators who have experienced various types of loss. Some lost loved ones to COVID-19, while others battled with their own mental health. When I think of the struggle being real, immediately, a particular colleague comes to mind; he lost his daughter in a tragic accident and exhibited an uncommon resilience, one that I found rare and hard to replicate. I watched him heal and process his loss with a positive spirit, inspiring others to overcome their own adversity. We are all confronted with challenges and losses, sometimes by choice but most often not. After all, who chooses loss and suffering? But it is our response to those experiences that define the outcome of our journey.

My life's work has been dedicated to education and instructional leadership. Within the world of education, teachers and school leaders are responsible for being fully present every day, maintaining positive relationships with everyone within our reach, and making important decisions in the short and long term. But what happens when we can't or don't want to? To whom do we turn? How do we mask and hide what we are facing? While we can't control what happens to us, we can control how we respond, even amid adversity.

John Maxwell, in his article entitled Leading through Adversity, beautifully articulates that *"going through adversity, though not pleasant in the moment, opens the door to new levels of influence. By staying poised and keeping a positive attitude under pressure, leaders can pass through adversity having grown in stature more than they ever could have in comfortable times."* Overcoming adversity creates resilience, maturity, greater opportunities and earns respect. Depending on the adversity we face, we have the unique opportunity to rise above it and thrive in our professional and personal lives.

Throughout my journey, I chose to fight, lead with love, and become the best version of myself. So, as you go through this book, know that whatever you are facing, you are not alone; know there is a village behind you and people standing beside you. They will help strengthen you and hold you up even when you think they are not there. Trust the process, honor your circle, and pursue what sets your soul on fire. Believe that better days are ahead, and go after them relentlessly and unapologetically.

Blessings,

Priscilla Mendez

I Loved The Way She Survived

"I loved the way she survived. Survival looked good on her. There were no dark marks under her eyes. Maybe deep inside, but I liked the way she looked through them and laughed at life. She did it gracefully. She's walked over glass and through fire but still smiles. And, honestly, I'm not interested in people who haven't lived and died a few times. Who haven't yet had their heart ripped out or know what it feels like to lose everything. I trust those people, because they stand for something. I knew what she'd been through. I wanted to thank her for surviving. And her to know she now had someone willing to stand with her too."

~ J. Raymond

Liberated

This week, my husband moved out. I anticipated an empty and eerie feeling within our home - kind of like when houseguests leave after a vacation. I imagined I would spend my time sobbing and grieving. Yet, to my surprise, I feel more alive and liberated than ever before. I feel oddly at peace, both in my heart and at home. For the first time in a long time, I smiled from the inside out.

It's incredible how much my relationship with my adult son improved in just one week. Over the last few years, our relationship was strained, and I sometimes thought he hated me. But last Sunday morning, as I was doing the dishes, he hugged me from behind, and it felt as if my weary soul had come back to life. I am overjoyed that this loss could lead me back to being physically and emotionally connected with my first love. I am looking forward to the journey; Without a doubt, I know it will be worth it.

Every night before going to sleep, I pray that this house will once again become a home. I am humbled by my little family's positive vibes, attention, concern, and unconditional support; they are the only ones brave enough to weather this storm with me. I am beginning to see each of them as the best versions of themselves - playing a unique role in my healing process. I lived in misery for so long, and now I suddenly feel worthy of the joy that comes with a new beginning.

As I tell my story and reflect on my truth, I am brought back to the first time 1 read Maya Angelou's expression of being free (in *I Know Why the Caged Bird Sings*) - She sings because she is free. Like that caged bird, confined for so long, I am ready to be free.

Gratitude

As an educator, I know firsthand how demanding this profession can be, and a global pandemic has only added unprecedented adversities to our already-challenging role. In my 20 years of experience, I have never felt such uncertainty and fear. Yet, despite the difficulties, I am filled with immense gratitude for teachers who push themselves beyond their limits to protect and educate their students.

It's heartbreaking to see how teachers can balance their own struggles and frustrations while serving their students. Although being around students brings me immense joy, I also feel sadness because I am mourning the loss of how things were before COVID. But I am fortunate to be surrounded by superheroes who don't wear capes, and their strength and resilience inspire me every day.

Despite my struggles, I remain dedicated to my role within the school. However, I haven't shared my new reality with anyone, partly out of shame and denial but mostly because my colleagues already have so much on their plates. As a school leader, I feel responsible for everyone's problems but cannot always share my own. Nevertheless, I keep a cheerful façade, smiling through my eyes even when my mouth can't. My focus remains on our students' academic achievements, and I hope my colleagues don't take a closer look and realize what I am genuinely facing. Because right now, it's just not the time to burden others with my challenges.

Your New Life Is Going To Cost You Your Old One!

It is going to cost you your comfort zone and your sense of direction.
It's going to cost you relationships and friends.
It's going to cost you being liked and understood.
But it doesn't matter.

Because the people who are meant for you are going to meet you on the other side. And you are going to build a new comfort zone around the things that actually move you forward.

And instead of being liked, you are going to be loved.
Instead of being understood, you're going to be seen.
All you're going to lose is what was built for a person you no longer are.
Let it go.

-Brianna Wiest

Opportunity

I t's amazing how our lives can change in an instant, whether it's unexpected or intentional. For me, those *words "I want a divorce"* shattered my heart, but they also brought a newfound opportunity.

Change can be scary, but it can also bring exciting possibilities. As I look back on my life, I see missed opportunities and lost moments. But I now have the clarity and drive to seize what's in store for me.

I'm reading, writing, and thinking about my future, designing it just as I envisioned it for myself. For too long, I was afraid to take action and pursue my wildest dreams, but now I feel a stirring [inside me] to do something impactful and leave a legacy. I want to change the world for women with similar experiences and tell my story instead of hiding it behind a smile. Life isn't always a fairy tale with a happy ending; I've learned that the hard way.

I'm no longer afraid or feel unworthy of life's blessings. I'm embracing opportunities that I once thought were out of reach (for me). It's amazing how something that once scared me the most has now allowed me to use my gifts and talents to their fullest potential. I'm seizing every opportunity that comes my way, and I'm excited about what the future holds.

Frustration

This past week has been especially difficult, as October usually is. The pandemic, fear, and uncertainty have caused stress and frustration to reach an all-time high for everyone around me. As a leader, I prioritize people, workforce engagement, and a healthy culture and climate. However, I feel deep sadness upon entering the school building because everything feels different. Schools are not meant to only be half-filled – schools are meant to be filled with children! The leadership strategies and tools I've acquired over the years now sit unused in my toolbox due to these challenging times.

When interacting with my colleagues, there is guilt when asking for their very best, pushing the envelope, and demanding high-quality performance. As a leader, this is my responsibility, but I am also human, and so are they.

Nevertheless, I refuse to lose sight of this, even on my worst day. I sense their frustration is getting the best of them, and I hear their complaints. I understand why they are frustrated, but the instability makes many of them lose sight of their why - their purpose. I notice the half-hearted smiles and waves, things that were once genuine and heartfelt. I cannot help but compare the present to the past, which puts me in a negative headspace. I wish I could turn back time and transport us to happier times.

Watching my hard work slip away is one of the most challenging things to accept. It's similar to how I felt about my failed marriage. These personal and professional feelings have left me feeling extremely frustrated and questioning [myself] why I am here and what the impact will be if this continues. The suffocating feeling of failure consumed me in more ways than one.

One bright spot remains - I am grateful for the children in our care because they made this week bearable. They are the only ones who make me feel like a superhero. Their hugs and waves literally give me life, even when I was at my lowest point as a woman and leader. It's critical for me to remember that despite the challenges, there are still moments of joy and fulfillment in my work, especially when I see the impact I have on these children's lives. I am grateful for that and will continue to strive for excellence, despite wanting to give up.

Worry

I find it intriguing how each week brings a new emotion as I adjust to the changes that have become my new normal in matters of the heart and life. Although initially, I felt liberated and unburdened when I decided to proceed with my divorce, I knew it wouldn't be an easy journey. I never expected this process to be effortless; however, surprisingly, the transition has been less challenging than I thought, but I've still shed tears and experienced moments of despair. I understand the harsh realities that come with separation/divorce, such as heartache, uncertainty, and brokenness.

As we draw closer to the end of this process, I worry more and more. Three main concerns keep creeping up on me. First, will I ever find love again? The kind of love that makes you feel like you're floating in the clouds, the kind that never fades. Does such love exist for me to discover? Second, will my children ever look back and blame me for this moment? Will the effects of divorcing and ending my marriage haunt them into adulthood? Lastly, will I be able to maintain our previous standard of living financially all by myself?

This week, I sought my mother's counsel in my time of need, and she reminded me that "fear is not of the Lord." I hoped she would offer the same wisdom she had while raising me. Although I knew in my heart that these fears were typical and part of the process, they were mine and mine alone to bear, no matter how many shoulders were offered. I suppose that anyone in this position faces these fears, but it's more profound when it's your reality. It hits home.

Despite my worries, there were some notable moments this week. I built a table, which is a big deal since I'm not skilled at following simple directions and have never built anything before. It was quite the challenge, with cardboard, white foam, and lots of tiny pieces (who needs all those pieces, anyway?). There were beads of sweat on my forehead, and it felt like I was constructing a house with my own hands. While the task was to build a simple table, the life lesson was profound. My best advice to you is to never rely on anyone more than you rely on yourself. I've learned this the hard way. While chanting my newfound mantra of *"this too shall pass,"* I'm working to ease my worries and continue my quest toward self-discovery. I keep hearing a small voice asking, *"Who are you? Whom do you want to become?"* In case you're wondering, I built the table without major injuries... this is certainly a good start!

Hopeful

Although we seem to have hit a wall regarding the culture within my school, I am still optimistic about the direction in which we are headed. Despite the typical murmurs and frustrations that arise in any school, I have been fortunate enough to be surrounded by greatness. As an essential worker during COVID-19 and an educator in general, I remain hopeful about our impact and what we have achieved at our school.

Perseverance has become more important than ever. I not only want us to persevere in our work, but I also need to exhibit this core value in my personal life. Perseverance is evident all around me. I see it in our educators who are facing extremely challenging circumstances. I see it in our students who struggle with limited interactions and hiding behind masks.

I am hopeful that our efforts to make an impact on our students will take root and positively impact them for years to come, even though most students are behind a computer screen. I hope we will improve our schoolwide performance, and my efforts will help move my beloved school to a place that reflects our hard work. As a leader, I aim to position those around me to do the heavy lifting, even if I am not present.

I envision a school that doesn't need me, and while this may be a scary concept, it will also be the moment I know that I have effectively done my job. I am also hopeful that I will find my way once I hand over the reins of our school to its new and eager leaders. Until then, my goal is to make each day count and inspire those around me, despite personal feelings or challenges.

The path to success is simple. You wake up each day and fight for the cause. You remain grounded in your "why" and show the world around you that there are countless opportunities that need seizing.

Balance

We have reached the one-month mark, and it's hard to believe that thirty days have already passed. In hindsight, I realize we should have done this sooner - we should already be at the one-year mark. However, fear, reservations, and pride prevented me from embracing reality and letting go, even though I knew our story had ended long ago.

Finding balance has become my top priority. I have buried myself in work for too long, using it to avoid conversations I didn't want to have and people I didn't want to be around. But in the last month, I have scaled back on the amount of work I do at home and learned that my role as a leader is not compromised as a result. In fact, finding balance has made me a more effective leader because I am in a better mental state.

I have found comfort in simple things like having dinner with colleagues and old friends, listening to music, and dreaming big. I have even started writing this book to document my journey, something I once convinced myself I didn't have time for. Now, I look and feel better than I have in years, and others have started to notice. When asked, "Is everything okay? You seem different," I often think, "If you only knew." Heartache, heartbreak, and loss manifest themselves in very different ways. One year ago, I cried daily, had bags under my eyes, drank too much, and felt lifeless. Fast forward one year, and it's almost the complete opposite; I feel fierce, strong, and grounded.

Years ago, I read "One Word That Will Change Your Life" by Dan Britton, and the word I chose was Balance. At the time, I had none and little desire to find any. Little did I know that I had to be brave enough to let go of what weighed me down to find and feel a sense of balance. While I wish things could have been different, I am content with what my life has become.

My daughter introduced me to the Broadway Musical *'Hamilton.' One* of the songs that always touches my heart is *'Look Around.'* I think it's because I always hoped that my marriage would be enough, the kind that lasts. While it didn't last as long as I had hoped, I'll keep these lyrics tucked in my heart and hope that one day these words will be my reality.

Look Around

Look around, look around at how lucky we are
To be alive right now
Look around, look around…
But I'm not afraid
I know whom I married
So long as you come home at the end of the day
That would be enough.

We don't need a legacy
We don't need money
If I could grant you peace of mind
If you could let me inside your heart…

Oh, let me be a part of the narrative
In the story they will write someday
Let this moment be the first chapter:
Where you decide to stay
And I could be enough
And we could be enough
That would be enough.

From the Broadway Musical *'Hamilton.'*

Tired

Have you ever felt like you're not allowed to be tired or fatigued occasionally? I know I'm guilty of that, especially in the workplace. As a leader, admitting I'm tired or drained can be seen as a sign of weakness, and I'm wired to suppress my feelings.

Strangely enough, I'm sleeping well, working less at home, and empowering others to step up and do the heavy lifting. Yet, it still feels like I'm not doing enough. I show up every day ready to give my very best, and it's rejuvenating to see students enter the building. I'm humbled daily that their parents choose us; I never take that for granted, but I often feel like I'm missing the mark (somewhere or possibly, everywhere).

However, I'm also exhausted because I'm bottling up this personal truth. There have been moments when I just wanted to let it all out and share everything happening to me, the person, not me, the principal. But instead, I smile through the hard parts and choose outfits and heels to mask how I feel inside. I've only shared my story with a few dear friends, and while I don't doubt that everyone will be supportive, I'm not emotionally ready to admit that I don't have it all figured out, even when I pretend like I do.

Leadership requires us to be actors and actresses - we're always on stage, front and center, often going off-script and "faking it until we make it." Even when we receive the worst news, we must wash it down before hosting an event or leading a meeting. It can be tiring, to say the least.

I'm weary, and I remember I haven't taken a vacation in years. I haven't done exactly what I want to do in forever. But I choose to believe that my time as a caterpillar has expired, and my wings are ready just for me. I'm ready to soar and show the world the newest and most dynamic version of myself.

If you're feeling tired, exhausted or fatigued, I encourage you to take care of yourself and recharge your batteries regardless of what you think needs to be done. For many years leading up to this moment, I neglected this, mainly by choice. But now that I am free to live, my body is experiencing cleansing and emotional restoration from all that was sucking the life out of me. The world is your oyster, and I know that your mind, body, and spirit will soon align and rid themselves of the tired feeling that has been weighing you down for far too long.

Bold

This week, I did something that some may consider unthinkable or unallowable: I got two tattoos to commemorate my new life. The first tattoo says "Fe," which means faith in Spanish. Faith is defined as complete trust or confidence in someone or something or a strong belief in God or religion based on spiritual apprehension rather than proof. At this moment, having faith means that I will overcome my current challenges and loss. I trust that my unwavering faith in God will see me through the hard times, even if I don't know what lies ahead. Although I feel both peace and uneasiness at the same time, I believe that my faith will help me get through anything. Have you ever trusted your faith more than yourself or those around you? It's a remarkable feeling that brings your mind, body, and soul serenity.

The second tattoo on my body reads, *"This too shall pass..."*. This phrase can be found in 2 Corinthians 4:17-18 and is something I whisper to myself every morning as I look in the mirror. I won't deny that there are moments when I feel afraid, alone, and stressed about my financial situation. But I trust God's promise is real and meant for all his children. Although the path I'm on is uncertain, I know there is light at the end of the tunnel. I believe I will one day speak my truth boldly and inspire many others like me. What was once embarrassment and heartache is now confidence and assertiveness.

These tattoos are symbolic in many ways. First, tattoos bring temporary pain, much like heartbreak. Second, they allow me to live by my own rules. Getting them was exactly what I wanted to do at that moment. I hadn't done something just for myself in forever. Third, I went with my adult son, whom I spent so much time judging for his tattoos. I regret that now. In this world and this short and precious life, we should offer love and acceptance, especially to our children. Tattoos are often an outlet to cope with pain, and his tattoos have been his way of expressing pain and telling his story. Suddenly, I understood that perfectly and was right there with him, expressing my pain and hope for the future.

I'm grateful for the opportunity to boldly share my truth with the world through my tattoos.

Inspiration

Have you ever felt guilty for not being at work, even if it was for a good reason? I attended a Leadership Conference this week that took me away from school. Typically, whenever I step away from the building, I feel guilty. However, engaging with other leaders and sharing our raw and real struggles caused by the COVID pandemic was a gift. This experience solidified for me that Leading Through Loss is a reality.

COVID has forced many leaders across the nation to lose something. During the conference, I collaborated with leaders who had lost parents, spouses, job opportunities, and everything that was once familiar. I stood among leaders battling depression, alcoholism, and deep-rooted anxiety caused by the uncertainty of the future. These are topics that leaders do not often discuss, especially with those whom they lead - after all, you are the leader! I felt humbled knowing that so many others were experiencing similar losses, some even worse than mine.

"Being a Light" was one of the themes of the conference. I have always advocated being a beacon of hope for those we serve. I wholeheartedly aligned with the concept of being a light for others. However, as I listened and tried to understand what was being said, I brainstormed ways to continue being a light and a beacon of hope during a time that has made many feel 'dimmer.' I do not believe that a leader's heart for the work changes or that our core beliefs change, but I do believe that shining lights illuminate differently based on the times and the situation you are facing.

A significant takeaway from the conference was a quote by Nick Vujicic, "You get paid to save lives. You have the best profession in the world." That struck me. I might not feel like the brightest shining light right now, but I am honored to do this work and to save lives. This is larger than COVID. This is bigger than our individual struggles. This is bigger than our own insecurities. This is what I will hold on to during these trying times. It is a tall order, but leaders, WE ARE THE ONES!

The pain will come,

Let it visit,

Cry it out,

Vent it out,

And ask it to leave.

Do not allow it to build a home and call it broken.

We aren't meant to be broken forever,

That is punishment to our hearts and minds."

~ Excerpt from HER Book by Pierre Jeanty

Lost

Lately I have been experiencing a whirlwind of emotions that have caught me off guard. I often ask myself, *"Is this real life?"* Well, yes, it is.

COVID has taken a toll on everyone; so too have the upcoming elections, and yet again, the nation is divided. Additionally, my personal truth has awakened me in a way that feels like I'm seeing the world with fresh eyes. At times, the brightness of the light can be blinding.

Although they say distance makes the heart grow fonder, I have not felt this. Nevertheless, I did see him [my ex-husband] for the first time in six weeks. The encounter was unexpected and felt awkward and uncomfortable, especially for our daughter. My instinct was to run and hide, but these past six weeks were a time of reflection and isolation that I needed.

This week, I cried for the first time. It was because of something seemingly small, a flat tire. But it completely rocked my world. For the first time, I realized that I was truly alone. There was no one to call, explain the situation, or ask for help. It made me feel utterly sad and moved me to tears. In that instant, I understood loneliness in a new way.

So, I did what any helpless soul would– I called him, and he came to the rescue. I was angry at myself for being vulnerable and asking for help, especially during this transition. The tire was fixed, and he was needed as he always had been. Having someone you can count on is such a beautiful thing. Having someone you can't make it work with is an utterly sad thing.

Life is filled with unexpected twists and turns, and feeling a range of emotions is okay. It's important to remember that we don't have to go through life alone; there is strength in asking for help when needed. I remind myself; this too shall pass…[right?]

Courageous

Good coaches don't wait until halftime to make changes when they notice that things aren't going as they should within the game. Likewise, as a leader, it's important to be proactive and make changes when things aren't going as planned. As we worked on school grade calculations this week, I realized that our school was not where it needed to be. Instead of waiting for things to improve on their own, I knew that bold moves were necessary for the benefit of our students.

Good leaders always ask themselves what they could do better. So, I asked myself, *"Why can't we get this right?"* It was clear that we needed to make changes, and fast. I knew it would be a daunting task, but I was willing to do whatever it took to ensure a brighter future for our school.

Making bold moves can be stressful, especially when the stakes are high. But I knew that I had to act and act quickly. With the support of my staff, we made necessary staffing shifts, had courageous conversations, and moved pieces to where they fit best. It was a challenging process, but it went much better than I imagined. I felt empowered and courageous.

Making hard decisions becomes more manageable when we put students first and remain true to our moral compass. I am grateful for the support and buy-in from my staff and for everyone rallying together to do whatever it took.

While I couldn't save my marriage...and can't make COVID go away, I am determined to make a positive impact and work relentlessly to save my school. I am committed to leading our school to greatness, and I won't stop until we get there.

Leaders, regardless of what you are facing, be courageous...be bold!

Questioning

I knew the moment would come when I began to second-guess myself. I found myself rethinking my decision and the urgency of it all. I learned that we all see and describe things through our unique lens. As they say, there is your side of the story, my side of the story, and then there is the truth. Whichever it is, I always hope to remain grounded in the fairest version of the truth, which doesn't negate our person or cause more hurt to an already hurtful situation. I have questioned my pride, stubbornness, drive, and inability to fully give myself to the institution of marriage. The few people that know what I am going through have asked, *"Why don't you just go back?"*

To answer that million-dollar question, "just going back" doesn't make sense for anyone involved. Honestly, it would be like traveling down an already broken road. Marriages and relationships affect and involve a husband and wife and affect everyone in their inner circle. However, I still question the future and what lies ahead for me. That is the scariest question of all. I question if I will ever be enough and if I need to be more. I've noticed that most men are turned off by women who have themselves figured out, are grounded in their profession, and value independence.

The complexity of these questions and the implications the responses will have on my future make me anxious. My best advice to myself and to anyone who might be feeling the same way is to stop being so forward-thinking for once and to focus on healing in the present. I'm unsure why I was so fixated on the future when I hadn't figured out the present. I am taking a deep breath, figuring out what I must work on, and focusing on ME! Perhaps I haven't met my match or someone as unapologetically fierce as I am. I know my perfect match exists. I believe he was created just for me. And even when I can't see or haven't met him, I know he exists!

Laser Focused

Last week I made some bold moves that required me to shake things up a bit. This week, I had to mobilize myself into action. It's a common misconception that a challenging home situation doesn't affect your work. But in reality, it can shake you to your core and make you act and feel differently. I've become an expert at masking my emotions, especially at work, which has become my escape. However, over the past few weeks, I noticed that I was walking a little slower, struggling with a cloudy mind, and constantly thinking about other things. I knew I needed to change that, and with conscious effort, I was starting to feel like myself again. It felt like a significant weight had been lifted from my shoulders, and I was walking taller, moving and shaking, and feeling extremely productive. That's who my school community needs me to be, and that's who they deserve.

One of my dear colleagues even complimented me by saying, *"You're like Wonder Woman and Super Woman at the same time."* It made me beam with pride because that's always been who I am and how I lead. I hope that amidst the chaos that school leaders face, they can give us a little grace and see us for who we once were, who we are now, and who we can be in the future. After all, leaders need grace too!

Disappointed

As I reflect, I realize that this moment in time is both a blessing and a curse. I pride myself on being a very private person, especially when it comes to deeply personal things. Over the past few months, I have shared nothing with those outside my small circle. I am grieving this loss in my own way while trying to maintain cordial communication with the Mr. [After all, we have a beautiful daughter that deserves nothing less]. Additionally, I am also attempting to reinvent myself without falling into a deep depression as I grieve this loss in my own way. It's not easy; truthfully, I am struggling because I am now alone.

I find myself disappointed in the things that once brought me joy and in the people who surround me. I wish people would show up for me the same way I would for them. Word has spread, yet no one has reached out to offer support. It is painful! I try to remain silent and isolated in moments of disappointment or where I could have reacted negatively. I have chosen to preserve what once was in its purest form and exercise tact. I gain nothing from speaking poorly about a person or situation that no longer suits me.

I came across a quote that instantly aligned with the way I felt. It read, *"It is the sweet moments of support we all want...when things get shaky, there's that one who isn't...that one who slips their hand in your pocket and says with a smile, I've got you."* That is precisely the kind of support I haven't had. Aside from my household and a sprinkle of confidants, I find that not everyone can be counted on. I shouldn't be disappointed by this, but I always am. This process taught me to be more present for those in need. I hope to show up with a kind word, a hug, or a bottle of wine. I hope I continue to see the good in others and never use my words to belittle what once was a beautiful story – nobody wins.

Unmotivated

I'd be lying if I didn't say that there were moments when I felt unmotivated and like my sense of direction was off. Like me, I am sure you have had days where you get out of bed not feeling quite like yourself but well enough to go to work and fight the good fight. Moments where you glance at your computer and stare blankly at the screen. Or maybe you look at your calendar and think, *"I really don't feel like doing that today."* Perhaps you've noticed it in your short, cordial, and detached interactions with others. I'm not too fond of moments like this because they do not align with my leadership style or my temperament. Not only are these moments not impactful, but they make me think the same thing all the time... *"Snap out of it. You should be doing more. People need you."*

I believe this stems from being overly tired, the realities of being an educator and leader during a pandemic, being human, and navigating my own inner struggles. As I go through the motions and think of the endless To-Do Lists and deadlines and brainstorm ways to keep everyone happy, a slight sense of defeat often creeps up on me...because sometimes, it's just too much. I wish my staff knew I am often overwhelmed, deflated, and unmotivated. I can relate to and understand them more than they will ever know. Being unmotivated is rare for me, which is a good thing. I need this feeling to pass quickly because schools and kids don't need unmotivated leaders or teachers. They just don't. And I will not be that person.

Fierce

For the first time in a long time, I decided to take care of myself. I feel stronger. I feel prettier. I feel alive. I have lost a noticeable amount of weight [which is not uncommon during periods of suffering and stress]. For any ladies reading, losing weight is always a bonus and a win! I am wearing things that have been tucked away for years, once seen as things of the past. I enjoy the compliments I receive, as they strengthen my self-esteem and hope for a new version of myself. I have committed to working out 3-4 days per week, and in those moments alone, I am pushing myself even though I am tired and weary. I enjoy the things that I am allowing myself to engage in daily. I realize I am worth it; YES, I am worth the effort. I am amazed by how nothing is falling apart because I gave up just one hour per day. In retrospect, I should have done it sooner. I vow never to forget about myself ever again. I took three pictures this week, and eye-opening is what they were. I almost didn't recognize myself. I compared these photos to those taken at the onset of COVID and gasped. I do not recognize the woman in that photo. Smiling but sad, overweight, and completely broken. I only know this because 'she' is me! I still have a long way to go, but I am confident I never want to be that version of myself again. I thought I was 'ok' back then, but the image in front of me shows the opposite. How can our self-awareness be so off-base at times? An excerpt from Courtney Peppernell captures it perfectly. *"A long time ago, she used to believe all the roads in the world would not lead her to where she needed to go. But she's older now, and she knows roads crack in the heat and disappear in the snow, but if she places one foot in front of the other, eventually, she will get to where she needs to go."*

Thankful

T hanksgiving season is here! With a heart of Thanksgiving, I walked the building countless times and marveled at the great things we have created collaboratively. I looked at once bare walls and smiled at the memories we have captured for all to see. I am grateful for the story unfolding and the pages that have yet to be written. I watched interactions between the students, and I'm so grateful for their love and their need for guidance. Because of them, we can do the work we are most passionate about. I am grateful for my colleagues and the fantastic things they are doing on behalf of their students. This is the most challenging time of the year, one which is taxing for school leaders – emotions are high, and almost everything said feels like a complaint or judgment. I wish my staff knew that my heart overflows every time I see them interact with our students and that I could not do this work without them. I am grateful for the families that continue to support us, even during a global pandemic! Surprisingly, I am grateful for my gifts and talents and how hard I push myself daily. I know that greatness is not a seasonal phenomenon – I know that great leaders not only show up each day but are the same person, walking the same walk and talking the same talk over time. This year, I am grateful for good health, a functioning school, and the future before us.

Blessed

Thanksgiving 2020 was one for the history books. I must admit, I was terrified to go through Thanksgiving this year since it brought such painful memories of a heartbreaking Thanksgiving from the year before. You see, last Thanksgiving, my daughter overhead her father and me discussing our divorce, and her world instantly shattered, as did mine. I cannot shake the sadness we all experienced that holiday season. It took a lot to rebuild ourselves and recreate a sense of normality despite our loss. For the first time, we did not have plans to spend the holiday with extended family, which also caused much sadness for me. Often, we think that being in a room of people equates to happiness, yet I'm sure we have all spent moments surrounded by others and still feel utterly alone. My vision for Thanksgiving 2020 was to create a moment, a moment for the

Fab 4, as I call us. We started the day with our annual Thanksgiving Brunch; I created a beautiful display to show my love for my little family. I often wonder if my kids love our traditions as much as I do. I think of a place and a world without those moments, and truthfully, life would not be the same. We enjoyed the Macy's Day Parade together, which was also very different due to COVID. It reminded me that everything changes and that being different doesn't necessarily mean it's bad. Dinner preparations were underway, and we set up a fancy dinner scene outside under the lights. We dressed up and took pictures where we smiled from the inside out. We then enjoyed a quiet dinner for four. Before our quaint dinner, everyone shared what they were grateful for, which made my heart happy. I promised them that the upcoming year would be more about them and that we would start a new journey and business venture. I knew God was listening and that this was just the beginning. I am truly blessed!

Unplugged

During the holidays, I always take vacation days to spend with my family. I never take time off during the school year, so I savor holiday breaks to maximize sleep-ins and make memories to last a lifetime. It was great turning off the alarm clock, going to bed whenever I wanted, and cooking our favorite meals. It's ironic because my job is to cater to others. Fewer emails were coming in, and I was also grateful for that. While I did no work and kept my laptop tucked away, I did think about work [a lot] and the upcoming weeks and months. I am so honored to be able to do the work I love, surrounded by exceptional students who constantly remind me just how needed I am. I know my life's purpose...I feel it deep within me and know my work here is not yet done. I am on a mission for kids...I always will be. While I enjoyed being unplugged, I was still brainstorming and thinking through how to make the greatest impact despite COVID, mobile learning, and life. I was excited about what lies ahead for our beloved school. However, I know I must maintain focus, speak with clarity, and continue to make others feel like they can soar. Have you ever wanted something so badly that it hurts? That's how I feel about leading my school to success. Remember the words from <u>The Mount of Olives</u> [Page 67] - *"If it doesn't consume your mind, then your desire is not strong enough," the man said. "It is not enough to simply wish for a thing and hope that someday it will show up at your door. You must hurt for it. You must feel empty without it and you must want it so much that you can see it every time you close your eyes. "If it burns in your belly and it is the first thing you think about when you awake, the last thing you see when your head hits the pillow, then it is a burning desire."*

Proud

At the onset of this journey, I knew that I would become stronger, not just emotionally and mentally, but physically and spiritually. I gave myself permission to unplug and do exactly what I needed to do for me. I read a piece by Oprah entitled, <u>Why Women Let Themselves Go</u>. In it, she wrote, "*Women aren't on their own list of priorities. After taking care of everyone else, they are always putting themselves last on the list, and often have very little left to give. There are many women who aren't living – they are just existing. This is a form of self-abuse. Women often wear exhaustion as a badge of honor. The challenge for women is that they must re-language what it means to be a wife and mother. If you don't take care of yourself, in the long run, you are harming all the other people in your life. You won't be the only one who takes the hit.*"

Who doesn't love Oprah? But I especially loved that I felt like that was written just for me. I felt this specifically: **There are many women who aren't living – they are just existing.** I am tired of simply existing. I want to thrive, not just survive. May achieving the feeling of being 'alive' be the goal for the next season of my life. I choose joy – not just for those around me, but also for myself!

Concerned

Returning to school after Thanksgiving Break brought about mixed emotions. While welcoming our students and staff back was great, I felt something else consuming me. Knowing that COVID cases have increased in recent weeks, especially after so many families gathered together for the holiday season, left everyone on high alert. Instead of focusing on how hard it is to push high expectations, genuinely smile, and continue normal operations when you are genuinely concerned, I worked really hard to have stability of mind and heart. Although we had more COVID cases than I would like to admit, and there were moments when I felt like I wanted to bury my head in the sand, I knew that would help no one. I reminded myself that I was responsible for responding to all situations. We can all see the bright spots in any situation; the decision is ours. Mindset is everything! Every great leader knows that whether dealing with a crisis or triumph, everyone is watching and waiting for your response or maybe lack thereof. As I searched for clarity, I found **8 Tips for Navigating Turbulent Times** (Source: https://www.randstadrisesmart.com/insights/blog/leading-through-crisis-8-tips-navigating-turbulent-times) that can help us with our perspective and mindfulness.

- **Leadership Tip 1:**

Find your anchor - The anchor keeps the ship grounded during a storm.

- **Leadership Tip 2:**

Don't go into hiding – In times of crisis, the best leaders make themselves highly visible.

- **Leadership Tip 3**:

Communicate openly and honestly – Strong leadership and frequent communication are crucial during difficult times.

- **Leadership Tip 4:**

Diversify your team – The best leaders surround themselves with a diverse team, which during turbulent times, can prosper and come out stronger in the end.

- **Leadership Tip 5**:

Create a 'Can-Do' environment – Address the crisis and continue communicating clearly about the work that needs to be done [while offering support along the way].

- **Leadership Tip #6:**

Customize Care – The world's best leaders know how to care for each team member.

- **Leadership Tip #7:**

Be an active listener – The best way to keep the pulse strong for your team or organization is through active listening.

- **Leadership Tip #8:**

Have a long-term vision and a short-term plan – During times of crisis, the team needs to understand what is happening in real-time and how it impacts the organization's future.

Preoccupied

W hile time has been on my side, I have felt more preoccupied than I ever have or even should be. There was so much going on all at once that it was hard to juggle everything. Between COVID, reinventing myself, and work consuming me, I found it hard not to be overwhelmed. The reality of watching people around me get sick and what I would do if I also got sick haunted my thoughts. 'What would happen if I were out? How will the school run without me?' Would this send everyone into a panic? Not sure why I preoccupied myself with these unnecessary thoughts. I mean, let's be honest, I know things could run without me. The primary role of negativity is to creep up and make us see and feel things we shouldn't. Being preoccupied isn't bad, depending on what you are preoccupied with or by. I consciously decided not to focus on " what if I get

sick" but on "How can I *keep myself healthy? Take your vitamins.*"
I instantly felt more positive! It's all about perspective!

Looking at my current reality, I am most interested in
becoming a better version of myself and proving that I can do it
all. Have you ever experienced the nagging little voice that
said, *"What if you can't do it all?"* There's negativity and self-
doubt again! No room for that in our lives! I refuse to ask
things of myself that don't make me better. I made some bold
moves toward reinventing myself – all alone. It felt good to
branch off and see that what I needed right now was me. I
have also been preoccupied with work as huge deadlines
approach. We are fast-forwarding to the planning phase for the
upcoming school year, which promises new possibilities. We
all need something to look forward to. I love planning and
developing action plans. I am a forward-thinker. This week, I
turn to Mary Frances Winters, who wrote, *"Don't become too
preoccupied with what is happening around you. Pay more attention
to what is going on within you."* Since I can't control the
uncontrollable, searching deep within myself is the perfect
point of emphasis. My heart is the keeper of the dream.
Triumph is and will always be the goal.

Overwhelmed

There are a few leaders who verbalize when they feel overwhelmed. In fact, a leader's charge is to manage their stress and that of others to create a sense of ease for the good of the group and the organization as a whole. Sharing that you are overwhelmed is a sign of poor leadership. In fact, most believe that good leaders should never be or say that they are feeling overwhelmed. By definition, the word overwhelmed as meaning *complete defeat*. That is not a good position for any leader to be in. Yikes!

I agree that leaders are human and turbulent times can cause even the most effective leaders to feel overwhelmed. I thought I was exhausted last week, but this week was even more challenging and, yes, overwhelming. Time for a pep-talk [yes, we all need them!] This week, I overcame feeling overwhelmed by talking myself through it. Yes, COVID cases crept up daily, and my anxiety for people was sometimes through the roof, but the goal remains the same – remain champions for kids!

In the days leading up to Winter Break, I prayed and hoped everyone within my reach would be healthy, safe, and well. This week, as I looked back at the 8 Leadership Tips I shared last week, I am drawn to **Leadership Tip #2.**

Leadership Tip #2: Don't go into hiding – In times of crisis, the best leaders make themselves highly visible. Although I have felt overwhelmed, I have positioned myself front and center, communicating the good, the bad, and the ugly. Parents and staff have been appreciative of the transparency and time spent. *"Nonetheless, great leaders don't hide. Instead, one of the ways great leaders demonstrate passion for their vision and strategies is by being 'front and center.' Whether times are good or bad, rolling along smoothly or roughly, these leaders remain visible and engaged in the process."* [mapconsulting.com]. One of the things I admire about myself is that I refuse to hide or give up – I know some days/weeks are more challenging than others, but I remain fixated on the concept that, 'this too shall pass.' I am certain that one day I will celebrate this very moment and say, *"Look at* *you. You overcame that. You're still standing. You're better and stronger because of it."*

Festive

I t's absolutely the most wonderful time of the year... The holidays are finally here! The decorations are up, the lights are twinkling, and the gifts have been wrapped. When I step onto the balcony and look around, I am grateful that the holiday blessings are finally upon us. Seeing the tree adorned with decorations hovering over the intricately wrapped gifts makes my spirit so much brighter than it was a year ago. I distinctly remember how I spent 'that Christmas Break' hidden under a blanket and crying my eyes out. Today, I can't imagine that that was me. I look at pictures from that painful moment in time and don't recognize myself – unhealthy, depressed, and lost. I never want to revisit that awful place. That woman from one year ago serves as a reminder that life happens to all of us, that our lives can be turned upside down instantly, and that we can weather any storm if we dig deep enough and find the strength to do so. While momentary sadness still exists from a failed marriage, I feel sunny inside and extremely proud of my progress. I am 'making it' on my own – able to keep up with my responsibilities; I feel pretty good about that! The last month has been filled with holiday movies, Christmas goodies, and blessings from others. While this holiday will be significantly different for various reasons, I feel festive and grateful for how we have all adjusted. The Fab 4 will gather around the table this holiday, making new memories and planning for the future.   In retrospect, it feels like a Christmas miracle. They say, *"Seeing is believing."*   What I see makes me believe that trusting the process leads to a more favorable destination. I've arrived at a place I didn't know existed, a place where I feel embraced with love and one that was made just for me.

Inspired

The last week before Winter Break was always hectic, filled with holiday parties, Secret Santa, and closing out grade books for Semester 1. Due to COVID, the way we celebrate as staff looked quite different from other years, but we intentionally worked to bring holiday cheer to all. One day this week really stood out to me, which made my heart sing. I was compelled to share my heart with my staff:

Dearest Team,

We have spent the last semester jumping through hoops, navigating turbulent waters, and overcoming hurdles that we never signed up for...phew, we made it! We are almost there.

We may be tired. We may be filled with worry and concern. We have all changed because the world around us has changed. Yet today, I *was so moved by **moments,** and I'm constantly being reminded of my WHY once again [yes, we all need the reminders]*

In one day:

- *We displayed a true sense of **COLLABORATION** through our 1st Annual Festival of Trees - I'm in awe of the creativity and teamwork. Traditions matter. This exceeded my expectations [I LOVE when that happens!]* 🩶

- *I hosted a Facebook live! I stepped out of my comfort zone and felt myself beaming with **PRIDE** as I boasted about our amazing school family! From the number of views we received, it's safe to say our followers appreciated the gesture!*

- *We **BLESSED** an 8th-grade student leader with amazing Christmas gifts - thank you to everyone who was able to make this happen for this amazing young man. He gave a little speech, and when he addressed me, I could barely see through my glassy eyes. I was so moved and inspired. Our students LOVE us and the role we play in their lives!*

- *We **SURPRISED** one of our beloved staff members and her family with amazing Christmas gifts. This was a top school family moment for me. This is what Family is all about! We show up for one another when it is needed most. Thank you to* *everyone who was able to help take care of one of our most selfless colleagues!*

- *We **CELEBRATED** with our Festival of Trees winners! They made it rain in the lobby with their winnings, and parents enjoyed the fun and camaraderie! Great job, team!*

- *We received Caroloke videos and **LAUGHED** at the creativity, dance moves, and amazing spirit of our staff.*

- *We captured **MEMORIES** to last a lifetime in photos!*

- *We **HONORED** our students with the highest diagnostic growth by gifting them bikes and certificates. Their parents jumped in the photos too!*

*Today was remarkable. Reread the bold words above - that's what it's all about. People matter. People before programs! **WE DID THIS**...even during a pandemic!*

I am so proud to be your colleague and PRINCIPAL! I needed it today. I needed the reminder. I needed to revisit my WHY! Sometimes, we find it in the most unexpected places! Please don't lose sight of that.

*The magic I **LOVE** so much about our school still exists. When it becomes hard to see and feel - I will help us find it. Today was a great day - and I am eternally grateful for it and for each of you!*

Nostalgic

This Christmas Season solidified a new beginning, and while it wasn't good, it wasn't bad; it was simply different. For the first time, I shared my daughter for the holiday and missed her even before she left. I felt guilty knowing that my table and heart may be filled in greater ways than 'His', this holiday season. Despite everything, I still worry about Him. I tried not to harp on those things as they would only make me sad. I intentionally focused on how blessed we continue to be, being grateful for our good health, and creating new memories within our home. There were no ill feelings – we exchanged gifts and still worked together quite nicely. I especially missed spending the holiday with my extended family [we are a fun bunch!]. I am secretly thankful that we are limited in how we gather because I am just not ready to face the crowd or explain anything to anyone. While it has been my reality for some time now, it remains painful. I watched the kids closely this Christmas – I searched their eyes to ensure they were doing fine. They are. They are loved, taken care of, and like the rest of us, they adjust in the most empathic way. It is true, children are more resilient and more honest than we are. They are also more capable of understanding and moving forward than most adults. There were many movie nights, eating fabulous meals at the dinner table together, and growing as a family. That was my greatest gift this Christmas! Nostalgia fills my heart, but so does peace.

Relaxed

I decided to take the entire Winter Break off, and I'm so glad I did. I started the break by sending out communication and promising our staff to unplug and disconnect for the rest of the break. I spent 16 days not really thinking about work, which was so unlike me that it caught me off-guard. I did spend a lot of time thinking about my future dreams and aspirations. Other than being a school leader, there are so many things I want to accomplish and things I want to gift the world with. There's a stirring inside of me that is larger than myself, a calling that is drawing me towards something greater, and a longing to take a huge leap of faith. My pastor has talked a lot about doors opening and closing, perfectly capturing what I am experiencing now. This ending is the closing of a door. This book is the opening of a door. I am fascinated by the idea that many more doors exist out there for me to open [and close]! I have allowed myself to step back from what consumes me [work] and use my free time to invest in things that fuel me. I was destined to share this message with others. I will not be afraid, as many of the words on these pages may be what someone needs to hear. While our stories are uniquely our own, we are never the only ones experiencing what life brings. Our bold truths are often intertwined with the truths of others. That creates a shared experience and connection with people we have never met. To everyone who shares portions of my story or experience, I'm so glad you're reading. You're not alone.

Pensive

Happy New Year – 2020 is gone, and a new year and new opportunities are upon us! Right before ending a very strange year, I reflected on the good, bad, and ugly moments of 2020. I know one thing with 100% certainty – I am in a way better and healthier place than I was just one year ago. Most people have a 'rock-bottom' moment that has shaped them or mobilized them into action. My rock-bottom moment occurred last New Year's Eve when my world was completely shattered, and there was no denying or hiding it. I had way too much to drink, followed by a 2-hour breakdown where I cried and wailed while everyone in the house looked at me in disbelief; their broken hearts reflected in their gaze. I now realize what an awkward position I put everyone in. I remember feeling compelled to go to church that night to ring in the New Year. I was still intoxicated and broken, but I knew it was right where I needed to be. Fast forward to this New Year's Eve... we had a Chicago-themed celebration for 4 [to remember our hometown]; we laughed, listened to music, ate together, caught a movie, and attended our church's online New Year's Eve service.   I was not inebriated. I was not sad. I was not broken.   My son joined us in worship. *Be still my heart.* Our pastor asked us to close our eyes and hold up our dreams for 2021.   For a brief instant, I opened my eyes and saw four sets of hands up, praying individually for 2021 and being a united front spiritually. It was the perfect way to end the year. It was symbolic and something that I had never experienced before.   What a difference a year makes – I'm eternally grateful for a meltdown-free, tearless, and sober New Year's Eve. The future seems more and more appealing now.

Clarity

Winter Break is just about over, and I have so much clarity about work and the impact needed to get to the next level. The stirring in my heart is greater than I'd like to admit. I recall opening the school year and talking a lot about my succession plan – I had never put any real thought into these things before. In retrospect, I realize this message may have caused uncertainty within my team. I believe it was a manifestation of the most uncertain time in my personal life and during an uncertain time in life in general. The many emotions I felt within forced me to speak of the past, present, and future. When I think about my WHY and what lies ahead, I can't help but feel an overwhelming sense of joy. I am laser-focused on the systems I must implement to achieve our desired state. I am mission-focused on cultivating leadership in others to help our school move forward. For the first time in forever, I can say that my mind and heart are aligned. I will always give it my all without compromising the desires of my heart. I love the idea of blooming where I'm planted – I've waited a very long time to feel this way. Thinking of the flower analogy, I envision all beautiful things beginning by planting a tiny seed. Whether the seed is a dream, a goal, or a new beginning, it can grow into exactly what we need. We must offer things like sunlight and water to see the seed sprout and grow. Instead of focusing on the storm or drought, the focus should be on that which brings life to the delicate flower. Our hearts are just like delicate flowers – fragile and quickly broken. To cultivate personal or professional growth, we must care for the things worth nurturing. I will tend to my garden [school] with the proper elements to see it grow. I will tend to my heart by allowing the sunshine in and watering it with words of affirmation and people who will help me flourish.

Content

The newness of being 'alone' is now gone. There is familiarity with how I move, live, and interact with those around me. They say it takes 21 days to form a habit – I have cultivated new habits and have fully embraced my separation. I have not cried since the tire incident. I have not mourned. I have not felt regret, as I know this is exactly where we must be. Sometimes the way we live depletes us so much that we have nothing else to give when it is done. We long for the person who once inhabited our bed, hoping that the 'spark' can be reignited. When it doesn't come to fruition, we become undone, and when the last embers finally die, what we find in that darkness is our self, which brings contentment. I walk with purpose. I speak with ease. I am focusing on today because tomorrow will take care of itself. I know so many technical things lie ahead of me [a divorce, custody, splitting what was once ours] and that makes me nervous, but I am content with the life that is unfolding before me. I'm working on mending my once-broken heart. This is a journey I have embraced and decided to follow where it's leading me. In the words of Dr. Martin Luther King, Jr. *"Faith is taking the first steps even when you don't see the whole staircase."*

Perplexed

Yet another memorable moment in time. We are a few weeks away from Inauguration Day, and evil has reared its ugly head once again. News coverage and social media show images of a divided nation. Sadly, it shows that we live in a society that has not come very far at all despite the progress made on the surface. Regretfully, we still live in a society rooted in systemic racism and hatred. My heart is heavy, and I am deeply concerned for the young people I serve. What will we tell them? How will we use this as a teachable moment? How will we channel our anger and offer unbiased teaching points and conversation starters? I am angry. I am tired. I am worried. I thought we were better than this. I pray for our Nation. I continue to fight the good fight. Spreading love and empathy. Respecting differing views and new ideas. Offering grace. Maintaining relentless hearts and passion for the work because the world around us leads to a broken road. It will take unity, love, courage, and leadership to pave the way!   Being a person of color is difficult in this society. As a Latina from a (very) Puerto Rican family, I was taught to stay quiet on these matters and to walk with my head down if it didn't involve me.   I worked hard to pave the way for myself, but now I realize the work is better suited to paving the way for others like me.

I can only imagine the way our young people are feeling. It is they who need champions and positive messages. I am certain that what I watched and observed as a current event is something I want no part of, and it challenges me to move toward my goals and aspirations. We are tasked with offering moral clarity on the events and the implications they will have in the days ahead, especially to our future generation that needs so much guidance, empowerment, and self-love.

Confusion

They say that every season comes to an end, and we often talk about the honeymoon phases coming to an end. I feel that this is my current state, and every new leaf I thought had turned no longer makes me smile from the inside out. I sense that the pressure of everything is finally getting to me. I am worried about things above me, below me, and beside me. I carry a load so great that I am forced to wonder, what is it for? Who will remember my struggles, wipe my tears or ease my confusion? I feel immense peace yet immense confusion. I am starting to feel like I am just going through the motions, like I'm more worried about others than I could ever worry about myself. I am living with a secret dark side – between monitoring my bank account, stressing over bills, and praying that my little family can live happily, something I deeply feel responsible for robbing them of for so many years. I stayed even when I knew I shouldn't have. I put on 'pretty pink glasses' and pretended everything was ok. When I rest my head at night and say my prayers, I pray for my state of mind and for the confusion that consumes me. I cannot see beyond today. I can dream of tomorrow but am too confused to develop a course of action.

Instrumental

I am thankful for the place I go to daily, the place that accepts me at my best and worst. A place that can offer me comfort when the rest of the world seems out of orbit. Tensions are certainly high in the world around me, but I see the amazing potential, which is what I love most about being surrounded by children. They are honest and filled with joy, and their comments are raw and pure. They remind me that it's ok to be open and honest. They remind me that making mistakes is completely acceptable and there's always someone in your corner who can make it all better [or at least try]. What made this week magical was working so closely with student leaders as we prepared for our annual leadership event. This is always my favorite time of the year. It is my favorite because of its positive influence on our school community. I realized I do not connect with our students as much as I should. I gained more from working closely with them in two weeks than I usually do all school year. I ask myself, *"How exactly does that happen?"* Together, we smiled, laughed, cried, and lived through our core values together. I am grateful that in this process and through leadership, others also positively influence me. Little do they know that they are giving me strength and courage during these extremely turbulent times.

Overcomer

I've had a lot of time to think and reflect on my situation and its negative effects on me. In retrospect, I find it silly that I became a woman I didn't recognize. It is unfathomable that I once felt like I was 'less than' and unworthy. They say that time heals all wounds, and I am uncertain if coming full circle is the result of time, accepting what is, or letting go of what needed to be left in the past. I have learned more about myself in half a year than I had during most of my adult life. I am confident. I am bold. I am happy. I am offering myself grace. I am grateful for the season that broke me and hopeful for the one that awaits me. I am in awe that I was able to maintain a life independently. I have exceeded my expectations and walk a little taller, knowing I am able, capable, and favored. There is no life without struggle, no heart that hasn't been broken, and no tears that haven't been unshed. Yet, I stand with my head held high, knowing that I have the opportunity to overcome and the mindset to thrive every day. My house has become a home. My dinner table is filled with conversation. My heart is filled with love. For anyone leading through loss, I challenge you to step onto the balcony briefly to reflect on your truth and determine how you will bloom right where you are planted. Whether by force or by choice, I can't get the following out of my head...*of all the roads she traveled, the journey back to herself was the most magnificent!*

Trusting

One of the most important leadership qualities is the ability to trust others. This is difficult because, let's be honest, some people are hard to trust. I strive to build trusting relationships and assume positive intent. I have consciously worked to put my trust in the work that others do without micromanaging, overshadowing, or hindering their growth. I notice that because of it, more people are shining and thriving. There have been increased opportunities for success and ease in how my staff moves and their interactions with students. I can't help but think that how we feel in our personal lives directly impacts our leadership. For example, as I overcome and prosper, I am better able to allow others to do the same. When I was in a bad place, I viewed those around me with eyes that were tainted. The darker my situation became, the more pessimistic my outlook toward others became. We often hold on to the notion that we 'must leave our problems at the door.' However, we are human, and sometimes our sorrow is greater than our ability to block out the things around us. I also found that I didn't trust myself enough to make it, especially during challenging times. I didn't trust that I wouldn't cry in the middle of the day. I didn't trust that I could learn from what was once the darkest moment in my life. I didn't trust that I could see my school thrive when I was falling apart. How could I trust those around me if I couldn't trust myself? Trust matters. Trusting others and trusting ourselves is a critical step toward authentic leadership.

Risk-Taking

All loss is associated with facing the unknown and taking a risk. Regardless of the loss we face, we sprint into action to combat the trauma we are facing. The effects of divorce are grave, especially on children and families. This was a massive weight on my shoulders, as I tried to anticipate when it would creep up and show the damage it could really cause. While these months of figuring things out have not been as scary as I anticipated, there were inevitable things that accompanied it. Keeping my home was my personal goal, so I took a risk and bet on myself. It was a long process, and scary to think that I would be the sole homeowner of my house. For so long, I was filled with self-doubt and voices that told me, 'I couldn't.' I honestly didn't think I would be successful and had visions of packing up our belongings and being forced to start over again. I think about those who lose it all, those who have to uproot their families and have no idea where they will go. I can imagine the stress it brings, as that could have been my stress. I've never been a risk taker, especially personally, but I am so grateful that I finally did. I appreciate the old life I built in my marriage and the role He played in helping me achieve my goals. I appreciate the heartbreak [never thought it would be possible for me to say that] that led to this very moment. I appreciate the risk associated with loss, as I've come to realize that I am stronger than I once thought. I will never second-guess what I can achieve or God's promise and favor in my life. Sometimes life has to get bad for us to experience the best parts of it. With my eyes wide open and head held high, I am ready to jump in feet first. What's the worst that could happen?

Emotional

As another school year comes to an end, I am in a place of deep reflection on the negative effects that COVID has had on our progress. Daily, I am filled with pride and admiration for those around me and the amazing things they have done for children. I am grateful for how we have persevered and remained a united front despite everything that took place. My worry comes from the unknown and its implications for our school. Something I am most proud of is that I have always led with my whole heart. Some of my greatest moments have taken place at my school. The role my school plays in my life is a very significant one. Recently, I was at a principal's meeting, and we were asked, *"What are you most grateful for?"* When it was my turn to share, I could not contain my tears. I simply started by saying, "Everyone in this room knows how much my school means to me. But I am tired of never making it [there came the tears] - I know we shine in other ways, but when the scores come, it doesn't show. I'm tired, guys; I'm really tired." I went on to share how grateful I was to my Area Director for her belief in my leadership and her unwavering vote of confidence. She helped me realize that I have always been purposefully placed and believed in me, even when she didn't have to. Perhaps I was looking at things the wrong way this whole time. Good leaders are also indebted to the leaders above them. As I closed out my reflection, I shared how badly I want our school to be a success story - not for me, but for her, our teachers, and our students – they deserve it.

Essential

When I think about the word essential, I naturally think of essential workers – I happen to be one. As I accept becoming head of my household, I now realize how essential I am on that front. I experienced some anxiety, as it is still so new to me. For all you married readers or those with life partners, be grateful for someone to share the load with. Life is so much easier when two people work in unison or toward a common goal. It has been the hardest part of this journey. I don't take my responsibilities lightly, but this has been magnified with the realization that I am 'it.' What I do or don't do will be the difference between success or failure, which affects everyone in my household - those I love the most. I could never let them down. There are moments when there is angst, worry, and a bank account that seems to diminish before my very eyes. I have always been very maternal and viewed as the family's matriarch – today, this holds truer than ever! I am grateful for the work that I do, the gifts and talents I have, and my deep-rooted passion and work ethic. I know they're counting on me, leaning on me, and rooting for me from the sidelines. The weight of the world is literally on my shoulders, but I am focused on walking in purpose and seeing my family thrive! I pray for favor and many years of life to love, protect, and provide for them. I will know I have arrived when I reach this milestone.

Misaligned

Over the last few weeks, I realized that I have often focused on the wrong thing – you see, accountability does crazy things even to people with the best intentions. Don't get me wrong; accountability is a top leadership principle and one that is necessary for all organizations. Without accountability, no organization would thrive, and adults would become complacent, which leads to ineffectiveness. I find that throughout this journey, I have been so focused on the outcome that I have overlooked the process. I have been so fixated on school accountability that I have frowned more than I've smiled. I have cried instead of laughed, and in certain moments I have caused others anxiety instead of being inspirational. High stress doesn't lead to increased accountability; it causes paralysis. It creates unnecessary pressure and causes even the most well-intentioned individuals to hit a brick wall. Feelings of being inadequate, or not being able to perform/meet the demands of the job consume every moment and thought. I know the dreaded feeling firsthand. It wasn't until I allowed myself to move forward and savor every moment of the journey that I began to see the magic and moments we create for the kids every day. I advocate for magic and moments [because people never forget them] but realize that my own stress and fear of failure have not allowed me to appreciate them for what they are. Long after I'm gone, I want to be remembered for what I was able to accomplish, not for what I wasn't.

Powerful

I am all about girl power, but like many women, I have taken a backseat in matters that I should have been more proactive about. For example, there are so many things I am clueless about. This issue stems from never having a male figure to teach me certain life skills, only to become a busy wife who didn't get a chance to learn them either. I didn't ever feel the need to. Have you ever felt this way? Fast forward to unexpectedly being alone and 'in charge,' and you're left alone with tasks that you didn't even think twice about before since you always had someone who took care of them. I have learned how to speak for myself, fix basic things, manage things financially, and make minor renovations to our house. This has taught me invaluable life lessons and required me to watch a lot of YouTube videos. Watching the outcome of home projects and being able to say I accomplished these once foreign tasks has made me feel powerful. These are silent victories. I am eternally grateful to the friends who stepped up to help and offered varying levels of support that I could never repay them for. Like most hopeless romantics, I was always on a hunt for my knight in shining armor, the man who would fix it all so I wouldn't have to. I had that, and it didn't help me in the grand scheme of things. Instead, it made me feel more hopeless as I embarked on life's journey alone. Moving forward, I want my daughter to learn life skills and how to do things typically done by men so that she will never feel powerless. I want her to feel powerful and accomplished especially if she suddenly finds herself alone. Remember my flat tire incident? That was a powerless moment. But today is a new day, and I have grown so much from that moment. **Change is inevitable; growth is optional**. I choose the latter.

Powerless

Am I the only person who feels like two different people sometimes? Like there is a work me and a home me. Ironically, my last entry on the home front showed signs of feeling powerful, yet on the work front, I felt powerless. I didn't feel powerless in a negative way, but I accepted that so many things were out of my control. It is becoming difficult to smile through the hard parts. I find myself wearing a frown as I reminisce about the normal life we once lived. There were magical moments, there were amazing events, there was a building filled with students, and of course, there were hugs. Daily, I watch as some of my most talented colleagues slowly become shells of themselves. They were frowning, too, and despite my best efforts, I felt I wasn't making a difference. I had to remind myself that they were also dealing with a lot, exhausted and stressed.

Internally, I wished I could shout loud enough for everyone to hear my message! "Remember your why. Don't forget about passion! You are purposefully placed! Our students need you! Our time is now! Rise above adversity!"

Some days they couldn't hear my messages of positivity or words of affirmation. Moments like those can really make you rethink things. I am hopeful for bright spots because they always come! In my moments of deep reflection, I came across something that resonated deeply with me. *"You can't skip chapters, that's not how life works. You have to read every line, meet every character. You won't enjoy all of it. Hell, some chapters will make you cry for weeks. You will read things you don't want to read; you will have moments where you don't want the pages to end. But you have to keep going. Stories keep the world revolving. Live yours, don't miss out."*

Encouraged

This year brought forth a rebirth on so many levels. I learned to exist in a once shared space, making it my very own and learning to play by my own rules. For me, this has been the best part of this journey. I very much like being in control of things [it's the leader in me]. I have come to the realization that I am what many would call an Alpha Female. By definition, Alpha Females embrace their confidence, and this helps them lead others. An alpha female tends to:

- believe her ability to achieve is limitless
- self-identify as an alpha female
- have a confidence that is contagious, which leads others to respect her as an equal
- showcase leadership characteristics
- be recognized by others as being impactful

- have extremely high ambitions

The term 'alpha' actually comes from research on animal behavior. Traditionally, it is used to designate the male animal that is the leader of a pack. These days, the term "alpha" has morphed. The more I read about the Alpha Female, the more I realize that she is me. I am she. While I embrace my leadership qualities and my ambition to soar as a leader, I also realize that I have given up a lot in my personal life. I ponder how this Alpha Female persona impacted my marriage and will likely affect my future relationships. On the professional front, being an Alpha Female helps me thrive. In my personal life, being an Alpha Female can repel those around me. I navigate this better professionally than I do personally. I've heard that I can be intimidating. I wonder if I am actually intimidating or if others are intimidated by me... there is a huge difference. One has to do with me, while the other has everything to do with them and how they feel about themselves. My ability to detach myself from others is both a blessing and a curse. I currently walk at the front of the pack with my head held high, but I worry that the longer I walk alone, the less aware I will be of my surroundings, and when I finally decide to look to the side or turn around, I will be walking alone. I have a profound complex – people see me as the best version of myself. I wish I could see it too! Because of the way I carry myself, it is perceived that I don't need anyone in my realm. This is farthest from the truth. In fact, I thrive on relationships and genuinely feel that people matter. I have mastered this professionally but not personally. I think that my failed marriage could attribute its demise to my own rise to success, losing sight of the true meaning of a partnership. They say that leadership is lonely – I ask myself, is leadership worth losing the things you once loved the most? Is it worth losing your ability to be vulnerable? Early in this journey [when I was hurt and angry], I blamed my ex-husband for ripping off the Band-Aid. Today, being in a better state, I question if my Alpha Female nature made him feel unequal or like he wasn't needed. I shudder, already knowing the answer to this question.

Doubting

T hroughout this journey, I have taken pride in my response to the situation and how I have continued to walk in purpose, knowing that this is exactly where I am meant to be. Have you ever reached your destination and known in your heart of hearts that this would be the outcome? I always knew that things would end this way, so while getting over this loss is difficult, I am not completely surprised. The only surprise is that it was he who ended things. The time has come to begin the divorce proceedings. Ouch! As expected, but not a fun discussion to have. I am grateful that we chose to stay away from attorneys and refused to fight. After all, it wasn't worth it. Instead, we chose to utilize the services of a mediator. The gentleman we worked with **was** cordial and made a difficult situation a little more bearable. We discussed dividing our shared assets, putting everything on paper, and planning for a life apart. There were several moments when I thought I would cry but didn't. I thought to myself, 'Well, this is it.' I also secretly asked myself, *"How does a couple actually get to this place?"* Not a single soul gets into a marriage preparing for it to end in divorce. After about 3 hours of planning for this new life and discussing the timeline, we walked to our own respective cars. What a long walk that was. I looked at the cracked pavement. For the first time in a while, I was filled with regret. Were we doing the right thing? In our post-discussion, we both agreed that these questions resulted from us wanting to find comfort in what was familiar and comfortable and not genuinely wanting to reconcile. The wait was on. I am fortunate enough to have children who seem accepting of the situation and have been fully supportive during the entire process. This also made things easier. As much as I want to bloom where I'm planted, I am filled with doubt and sadness. *"Nothing lasts forever"* – I hope that those words apply to how I am currently feeling.

Exhausted

T he school year has come to an end – we made it! While the close brought overall feelings of success, happiness, and looking forward to the summer holidays, I felt immense sadness that it had ended. Why have I been so sad lately? While there were many wonderful moments [because those always exist], it just wasn't the same. My colleagues [bless their hearts for their efforts] seemed completely over our school and were very apathetic. It's hard to watch your head cheerleaders frown and slump. It's hard to listen to your positivity warriors convey messages of frustration and questions whether this profession was even worth it. I was so grateful to have everyone out of the building. I needed a breather as much as they did! I needed time to process what was in my head and heart. I needed time to forgive myself for not being able to rise above the struggles brought on by COVID-19 fully. I'd like to think I did my very best under the circumstances, but the lackluster response from our staff is one that rings loudly in my ears.

The end of the 2020-2021 school year occurred exactly as my divorce began. Oh, the irony of that. My marriage ended at the same time as the most challenging school year to date. Something happens in your soul when you feel defeat and failure on both fronts. I am exhausted. Struggling for just small wins at work and at home sucked the life out of me. Like a caterpillar, I will build a chrysalis and emerge brand new. As they say, *"New beginnings are often disguised as painful endings."*

Struggling

Remember earlier in this story when I mentioned 'wanting to prove a point?' For the last ten months, I have held my head high and worked very hard to keep our lives intact. I was so grateful that I could offer stability to our little family. If I haven't said it before, I will now. This is hard! There is nothing easy about having sole responsibility for a household and lifestyle. I refinanced my house – I did it! With that accomplishment comes BIG financial responsibilities. Sometimes our blessings can be our biggest challenges. I am still learning how to figure things out, plan and stick to a budget, and accept that I no longer have a life partner to share the load with. That is one of the hardest things for me to come to terms with. I've mentioned selling the house to my kids several times, and my daughter is not a fan of the idea. You see, this house represents her life and is something that brings her comfort and peace. She has handled herself with tenacity and grace. She has accepted that her dad and I have ended; she splits her time and attention between us both and continues to thrive at school. Yet somehow, she cannot process losing this house. All she wants is for something to remain the way it was. For her, this house is it...sounds like the pressure is on for me! We are moving right along, and I'm making it. [sometimes, barely]! To date, I am surviving, not thriving [yet]. I look forward to a new season and a new beginning.

Over-It

Have you ever been let down by people around you and felt like you just couldn't get ahead? This summer has been a whirlwind, to be honest. We have had more resignations than I would like to admit. Like any reflective leader, I question what the underlying issue is. Is it me? Could I have done more? Have I cultivated an environment that people no longer want to be a part of? In each of these conversations, there are messages of gratitude, the 'it's me, not your reason, moves to other counties and schools, and people leaving the profession entirely. While each reason is valid, and I respect and understand them, it is still difficult. Every season must come to an end. However, it makes me doubt my leadership and question if we will ever get ahead. It feels like we take two steps forward and three steps back. I wish my colleagues knew that I'm just as tired as they are, that I doubt myself daily, and that maybe my season is coming to an end as well. But then again, leaders don't have that luxury. Instead, I reply with understanding, kindness, and well wishes. Some resignations hurt more than others. The effects of COVID have declined dramatically in recent months, but the ethic and drive that was there before has changed. I have a lot of hiring to do, plans that need to be altered because of the loss of key players, and thoughtfully planning my own messaging to kick off another school year. Of course, it will be filled with positivity and making it the best year for students, but as of late, I'm just over it. I can't shake it or deny it right now.

Transitioning

I often ask myself how time has gone by so quickly and how it has also healed my once broken heart. My heart has undergone transformation and healing. How have ten months passed me by so gracefully and unapologetically? I look at myself in the mirror [a lot], and the truth is, I have seen different versions of myself in the process. I have seen both the very best and the very worst versions of myself. I received my mediation documents for review, and I felt like the rug was pulled out from under me [even though I knew it was coming]. While this was the moment that clearly drew a line in the sand and closed a chapter, I don't wish to reread it, it served as a reminder that loss [all loss] does something to your spirit. The hardest part was being reminded of failure, the inability to fix it, and admitting that the end was near. To see my daughter's name on the paper as part of a detailed plan instantly shattered my heart. I am stronger today than I was at the onset of this journey. Had I known that this is where I would be today, it is likely that I, too, would have done things differently. Soon, I will be a divorced woman in a world I don't know how to navigate. The last time I dated, dating websites weren't the norm. Where do you even meet people these days? [Inquiring minds want to know!] As I enter the final stages of my journey, I choose love, both at home and at work. I choose to have a positive outlook on life and love. I choose to rebuild what was once broken. I choose to smile even when it is difficult. Most importantly, **I choose 'ME.'** I choose to fulfill my wildest dreams - in fact, I am running toward them like my soul is on fire. I've suppressed them for far too long and learned that life is too short to dwell on endings – focusing on new beginnings is so much more beautiful and promising.

Uncertainty

When COVID-19 started, leaders invested a significant amount of time and effort into their stakeholders and developed plans for how they would serve them and keep them safe. In my case, as a school leader, the emphasis became on our students, staff, and the families we serve. During a training I attended, a colleague shared something that really stuck with me. "Check on your principal friends because not all of them are going to make it." Those words resonated with me because we never talk about the 'not making it part.' While this leader did make it through COVID-19 and personal adversity, I am mindful of how it has affected me over the last year and a half. It is now Back to School season after a summer of unknowns. Unlike any other year during my leadership, we had a record-breaking number of resignations. This greatly affected me, as people are what matter the most in this work. It felt like the work being put in was constantly changing and in need of updates since staffing changes occurred almost daily. I am conscious that people don't quit their jobs; they quit their bosses. I question whether it was something I did [or didn't do] that has led us to this place. I know that regardless of who goes or stays, the work continues, the mission doesn't change, and we will be ready for normal operations on Day 1. This summer taught me that all plans need altering and that, in the end, everything will work itself out. It always does. Leaders, amid the storm, we have to get up, dust ourselves off, and try a new strategy to achieve greatness.

Acceptance

I t's hard to believe that nearly one year ago, I was mending fences and picking up the broken pieces of yesterday. It's hard to believe that I settled for a miserable home life because I was afraid of what others would say or think of me. It's hard to believe that I once thought that my happiness was less important than everyone else's. It's hard to believe that one year later, I have come to terms with what separation and divorce bring. I am so grateful that I decided to accept the implications of the road we were traveling on and mustered up enough courage to finally say goodbye - I always knew that had to be done. I am uncertain how one year can go so quickly and offer so much growth and healing. In most recent times, I've sat through mediation and maintained a grateful heart that the main focus has remained true – our daughter's well-being. I am happy that there is nothing to argue about, nothing to contest, and nothing left to fix. While the end of the road is near, the stage of grief I am in is acceptance. This makes the most sense for our family. When I sit and think about the finality of the matter, it is easy to become angry. But I quickly realize that resentment and anger steal my joy and aren't worth compromising my mental state or positive spirit. I accept being alone and am literally learning how to navigate a life I haven't known in many years. I am better because of it, and I hope that anyone in a similar situation realizes that painful endings also bring opportunity. Accepting that my marriage didn't result in a happily ever after and that knights in shining armor look differently than portrayed in movies has humbled me to look more at myself than to point the finger at someone else. I fell short. I played a huge part in this broken marriage. I could have done better. I should have been better. I now know better. I choose to focus on me, and because of that, I know that my heart and soul are on the mend. Thank God, because the angry version of myself was not becoming. This new beginning is more about me and less about anyone else. All because I accepted what was, what wasn't, and what would never be.

Joyful

Summer 2021 was filled with so many wonderful moments. With a small group of key players working over the summer, there were so many opportunities to build the team, laugh, plan without interruptions, and establish a vision for the future. Schools are interesting places during the summer. The students are home, deep cleaning occurs, tired teachers are enjoying their well-deserved vacations, and school leaders go into 'beast mode,' intricately planning for a successful school year. Summer planning is one of my favorite times of the year because it allows you to offer yourself grace, reflect, and forgive yourself for every mistake you made during the previous year. There is always the opportunity to pause and start anew. If only life and relationships offered us the same opportunity to reset and begin again with a blank slate. I love the idea of a blank canvas and being able to write the pages of a new narrative, year after year. I am encouraged by new beginnings. I am resting well. I am enjoying dressing in casual clothes and rolling up my sleeves to plan for an effective school year. While COVID-19 continues to be something on our minds, we now have the wherewithal to establish protocols, strategies to communicate effectively, and the experience to navigate what was once unchartered territory. Knowing what to do and how to do it is half the battle. What could possibly go wrong? I am claiming that the joy I feel about starting anew will bear new fruit, and the unwanted memories will be just that!

In Over My Head

Remember my reference to 'not all superheroes wear capes?' Well, I have tried to play the role of one for one year. While I don't wear a cape or need one necessarily, I admit that starting over is not for the faint of heart. The things that I am most grateful for, like being able to maintain my home and lifestyle, are also the things that stress me out most. It's just hard. It's different. It's exasperating at times. I have not been used to financial struggles in a very long time, and the adjustment has been painful. In my own silent moments, I wonder if my quest for thriving is a conquest to prove a point or the true desire of my heart. Is it worth struggling this much? I know brighter days are ahead, but I often feel like I am not living. I am working so hard just to survive. For one year, I've become my own hero – I hope I've become theirs as well. The truth is, if there were no one depending on me, I would have walked away and truly started a new life. A simpler life. A life where memories matter more than what meets the eye. While there are moments when I feel like I am in over my head, the reality is that I am abundantly blessed and take pride in being able to learn a new way of living. I know my kids are watching, and I pray they are as proud of me as I am of myself. They are and will always be my reason for pushing through.

Prepared

Summer is officially over, and our preparations and plans are now ready for execution. Our teachers and students are returning to school, which excites and scares me all at the same time. For as long as I can remember, 'first-days' always give me jitters. With my staff, I am always filled with anxiety around my Back-to-School messaging. A simple "Welcome Back, I'm so glad you're here" just isn't enough. Every year, I work to tailor a message that conveys my heart and where we are headed as a learning community. I write, erase, rethink, and overthink. While I probably take way too much time thinking about my message, I feel that those in front of me deserve to see and feel my heart. They need inspiration and motivation before the work gets hard, because it always does. This year, I struggled with what I would say and why. Being in the same building for the last seven years, I have come to realize that no one wants to hear a recycled message. So, I did the unthinkable – I shared my heart and my truth. I still can't believe I did that. For as long as I can remember, I have built this image of being unstoppable, unphased, poised, and confident [remember, the Alpha Female thing?]. Instead of being center stage as 'the leader with all the answers,' I chose to be a vulnerable woman – I chose to be me. In fact, I read the first few pages of this book. I didn't cry. I shared my reality and how I have led through loss over the last two years. It was liberating and taught me that my story is worth telling. I think back to the days when I couldn't fathom sharing that I was getting 'divorced.' I didn't want anyone to know because I felt ashamed and like a failure. Today, I don't feel that way at all. I'm just a person who happens to be in a leadership position, but I, too, face struggles and ugly truths. This was a huge step for me. I never want to return to a time and place where shame superseded my ability to be real. I'm facing a huge loss – so what? Isn't everyone in one way or another? As I ended my poised read-aloud, I felt the invisible "mic drop" moment because, for the first time in a long time, I felt free. Freedom to share looks and feels amazing! If sharing my loss inspires at least one person, then it is worth the vulnerability. It took me two years to get to a healthy place, and I am so glad I'm here I think they were too!

Secure

The divorce paperwork has been filed, the mediator served his purpose, and I am weeks away from officially being divorced. Sitting in the same room with the person you vowed to spend forever with to discuss the end is far from fun. In fact, it's heartbreaking. While I didn't cry, I kept thinking to myself, "Gosh, how did we get here? What could we have done differently?" There were moments when I looked over at Him and saw glimpses of who I fell in love with. I saw sad eyes and an overly quiet version of himself. I wondered if he, too, was having the same thoughts I was. In the moments where we discussed our daughter's future and our role in it, I felt overly positive; I wore a smile, maybe even a smirk. While a sad reality, my heart danced, and I felt secure in the decision we both made. I spoke with ease and confidence and signed each legal document with my most confident script – why shouldn't I? I know that one day I will rebuild my life and cultivate something with someone who chooses me over and over again. I will find my person. While I am not callous to the situation, I am certainly not the same woman who had to be scraped off the floor that one New Year's Eve. I did not weep or wail over the fact that the end had arrived. Instead, I am grateful for what once was and that I chose someone who has a heart for doing what's right. Do I wish that the ending would be a happy one and that this book topic wasn't one I would write? Of course! But life happens. People grow apart, and sometimes what is broken just cannot be fixed. I commend Him for standing up for what he believed in, and despite how painful it initially was, he saved us both. He saved us from continuing to live a loveless marriage, and because of him, we both have a fighting chance to truly be happy. We both have the opportunity to smile from the inside out. I came across some words that permeated my soul: **One Life. Just one. Why aren't we running like we are on fire toward our wildest dreams?** And that got me! That's the kind of existence I want to live. Because of him, we can strive for that without compromising a single thing. Sometimes ripping the Band-Aid off is the most painful part...but then the wound heals. I feel secure in our decisions, our plans for the future, and our quest to spread our wings. The lingering scars are gentle reminders that the other person was once there and part of the process – I am so grateful for healing nicely. I am forever grateful to the brave man who broke my heart but also the one who gave us a second chance at life. Here's to making the rest of our lives the best of our lives!

Renewed

Remember those feelings of excitement for the onset of an amazing school year I shared? Those have been replaced with fear. You see, COVID-19 has reared its ugly head again and has impacted our school community in the most unrelenting way. I am watching our staff and students fall ill, and it's become overwhelming, to say the least. My dearest thought partners and I spend most evenings venting and sharing our frustrations on our drives home from work. It is difficult to watch your plans come to a sudden halt, which you, the leader, cannot control. I feel helpless most days. Like most school leaders navigating this untamable beast, I spend most of my time sending COVID communication and working to cover classrooms. I smile through the hard parts and am under the most unexplainable pressure. Every night, I pray that I don't fall ill too. This causes profound anxiety. I find that the implications of this illness are far from being over. I wonder how we can move forward when every day feels like taking ten steps backward. It is only the second week of school, and I am exhausted – we all are. Everyone is sacrificing so much, and we are all terrified. I see it in our interactions, our hesitance to approach one another, and the quiet moments when we feel we don't have the answers. A beloved staff member recently told me, "No one gets slammed as much as you. But you handle everything so well, and I love you for it." That's the perfect way to put it. School leaders, teachers, and staff are still swimming in very turbulent waters. All we want to do is educate our children. Love them. Guide them. Nurture them and live our dream. Education is my true passion – one of my first loves. For anyone feeling this way, it is critical to find that bright spot, the very thing that brought you to this profession. That beautiful why will see us through. We may ask, "Will we ever bounce back from this? Will we ever be reminded of who we were once upon a time ago?" The answer is yes and no! Yes, we will bounce back from this new way of living and will have developed tools and strategies to make us better and stronger. No, we will not be the 'same' ever again, which isn't necessarily a bad thing. We are growing, evolving, and reinventing ourselves. Our new selves could possibly bring us moments as our best selves.

Conflicted

I t's Labor Day weekend 2021. Labor Day weekend. I happened to turn 40 this weekend as well! While there was no big celebration and fanfare due to COVID, I felt so thankful for good health and the ability to live my dreams. I find myself conflicted because while I am filled with gratitude, I also feel empty. I yearn for more, but I am unsure what that looks and sounds like. There's something about turning 40 [or any age for that matter] alone that can really make you put things into perspective. While I wholeheartedly believe that the world is my oyster, I have little clarity about what that looks like. Solitude is a scary thing, and the mind can play tricks on you. I am most grateful for my little family, who make me feel like I'm enough, not on my birthday, but always. This birthday, I received an amazing gift – a new baby niece to love! She is a reminder of new life, of all that is pure and beautiful! While we share the same special day known as our birthdays, I am committed to doing great things so that she, my future little Latina, will be able to enjoy it. I don't know if I am happy or sad. Fulfilled or empty. Maybe I'm everything in between. Here's to a new season, where clarity will be mine soon! Face reality as it is, not as it once was or as you wish it were.

Unfulfilled

While other authors often know their readers, I feel like you know me personally, having allowed me to share the innermost of my thoughts with you.

The first month of school has been the most challenging I've ever experienced in my 20 years in education. I am a woman of passion, and my love for my profession is evident to all who meet me. The fact that I must dig deep within myself to feel happiness is weighing heavily on my heart. Some days, it is difficult to get out of bed and fight the good fight. I miss the old days. I miss the memories we once had. I miss a more normal way of life. I miss hugs and not hiding behind a mask. I miss leading like my soul is on fire. Prayer works. When I can't shake the feeling, I resort to getting on my knees and letting God take care of it. I don't see it now, but there's a stirring within me that only He can provide clarity on.

Closure

Every good story has its end – I have gotten to the end of mine. My divorce is final, and it happened in the most unexpected way. There were no arguments, no need to appear in court in person, and no real moment of closure. I knew the moment I asked Him about the divorce that I probably wasn't ready for the response. "We've been divorced." That hit me like a ton of bricks – to think I was divorced for two weeks and didn't even know it is mind-boggling. Nothing felt different. Nothing changed. Nothing improved or worsened. At that very moment, I knew that I was purposefully placed and that my reason for writing this book as an outlet and as a method of healing was now coming to an end. Throughout this journey, I have faced amazing highs and unexpected lows. I have learned so much about who I was, who I am, and who I have yet to become. There have been moments where I've lost my way, feeling like a captain lost at sea. There have been liberating and empowering moments, allowing me to feel worthy of all life has to offer. My children are thriving, and in a rare moment, my son shared that this last year has been the happiest he's been in seven years. That broke and healed my heart at the same time. Reader, I encourage you to always strive to be the best version of yourself and to give yourself grace when faced with any kind of loss life brings you. In closing, I leave you with this, which I found while scrolling through Facebook! These words culminate in my journey and the way I view myself within the world and my new beginning.

She Woke Up Different

Done with trying to figure out who was with her, against her, or walking down the middle because they didn't have the guts to pick a side.

She was done with anything that didn't bring her peace. She realized that opinions were a dime a dozen, validation was for parking, and loyalty wasn't a word but a lifestyle.

It was this day that her life changed because she finally realized that life is way too short to leave the key to her happiness in someone else's pocket!

Reflective

I wish I could say that education and school operations have stabilized – they have not. The effects of COVID will be with us for years to come, and I am constantly mourning the loss of what once was. How do leaders lead through loss? In my case, my loss has been two-fold – I lost a former part of myself and what I once thought would be mine forever. I have also lost many of the amazing things I've worked toward as an instructional leader. I know I am not alone because leaders are people, first and foremost. Hidden fears, insecurities, doubts, and moments of questioning are the truths leaders don't share. Leaders lead through loss because there is no other choice. I have been blessed to be chosen to lead and change lives, which has given me some of the best years of my life. Although my shine isn't as bright as it once was, I know my Why and my deeply rooted passion for positively influencing people. On days where I lose sight of that [because I have], I remind myself of my worth and value. I remind myself that for as long as I lead, I must do so with my whole heart. I have ventured into the University realm and am teaching education courses! Those moments are magic and allow me to shine in a different way. Another layer to leading – another opportunity to make a difference to shape aspiring teachers to be amazing for kids. This isn't the end of my leadership journey but another form of leading. Reflection and soul-searching keep me grounded and honest with myself. Leaders, remain faithful to your moral compass, grounded in your why, and relentless in your how! The rest of your story and legacy depends on it.

Manifesting Wins

Now that we've established that love and loss are part of the human experience, and that none of us are exempt from feeling the highest highs and the lowest lows that they leave imprinted in our hearts and souls, it's time to begin thinking about how we move forward, becoming the best version of ourselves. Personally, I've battled with this part because I was unsure how I would exist in a world unknown to me. I chose isolation to avoid discussing painful truths. I pushed people away, fearing that they would judge me, as I was judging myself. In moments of sadness and depression, I forgot every leadership technique I had ever learned. Trauma and loss have the ability to completely make us lose ourselves. But those days are over [but still an uphill battle]. I am still working on becoming precisely who I want to be.

I am most proud of the fact that I am sharing my story and have mustered up enough courage to talk about it, using it as a valuable lesson and, most importantly, growing from it. In my current season, I am actively working on manifestations for my life. In an effort to protect my spirit, mindset, and energy, there are several intentional [and practical] things I've learned to do to protect my peace. Several things have occurred that had the potential to take me back to that maddening place – the place I was in at the onset of this journey. My now ex-husband has completely moved on in every sense of the word. I have moved on to a different school to lead a new school community. I've dealt with both in the following ways:

While knowing your ex has moved to a place called happy is initially a tough pill to swallow, I have chosen to focus on the positives. His relationship with our daughter is strong, positive, and consistent. We are excellent co-parents and are in each other's corners, no matter what. I remind myself that the relationship ended for a reason, and I am committed to never making the same mistake twice. I honor the high points of the relationship and partnership that once was and accept the fact that it no longer served us. I choose to celebrate other people's happiness instead of being bitter, as it is only damaging to me. I refuse to compare where I am to where he is, as every journey is uniquely it's own. Acceptance has been a game-changer for me. I wish him the happily ever after that I wish for myself.

Professional journeys are exactly like personal ones – they all have a beginning and an end. While my professional journey ended at a place that I loved with all my heart, I actively chose to change my mindset on how I viewed this loss. Yes, I cried – a lot, as did my staff. Initially, it's like losing a loved one; it brings a sense of loss. But it also brought such great opportunity, personally and professionally. I hold the most beautiful memories made at my old school deep within my heart. I am a forever cheerleader and supporter. I am comfortable with what I was able to accomplish [as well as those things I wasn't able to accomplish]. I also know that I am better off having had that experience. My new beginning came at a time when I needed it most. I smile every day. I have met amazing people. I am serving with my whole heart. Endings bring new beginnings…I now accept them with open arms, an open heart, and a positive perspective.

By definition, manifestation is the transmutation of thought into its physical equivalent. It's the process of taking an idea, a dream, a goal, or a vision and taking the necessary action steps to make it a reality. Anything you can daydream about, you can create in your life. This has been a game-changer for me! In a place of happier and healthier, these simple processes have changed my life!

1. Positive Affirmations

As a leader, positive affirmations have always been a natural part of my leadership style. I value using positive affirmations with my staff and do it often. I am mindful of the human experience and know that the world needs more positivity. I use positive affirmations in just about everything I do; however, I use them for others – not for myself. I've used them to uplift others but somehow forgot about myself. After looking in the mirror, [literally and figuratively], I realized that someone significant [me] was also in need of positive affirmations. Rather than waiting for someone to provide me with positive affirmations, I have been committed to offering this gift to myself. An affirmation consists of words or phrases used for a positive situation. They are words that help us get through difficult times. They help keep stress levels down. Positive affirmations have helped me feel more positive and in control of my feelings. This didn't feel natural at first because loving on myself was not part of my practice! But now I remind myself that:

I am loved. I am bold!
I am beautiful!
I am different and unique!
I am unapologetically me!
I am worth love and respect!
I am a work in progress!
I am always growing and changing!
I am powerful!
I am worth fighting for!

These simple affirmations are a daily reminder of my worth and truth. They are the words I have gifted myself with. What are your positive affirmations?

Reflect on your own self-talk and inner dialogue. Are there any negative or self-limiting beliefs that you frequently encounter? How can positive affirmations help counteract these beliefs and promote a more empowering mindset?

List at least 5 positive affirmations *(aligning them with your goals and values). Incorporate these affirmations into your daily routine to reinforce positive self-talk and build self-confidence.*

- ☐
- ☐
- ☐
- ☐
- ☐
- ☐
- ☐
- ☐

2. Permissions

I have always been an avid reader; quite frankly, I love getting lost in a good book. I stumbled across a book that has changed my life. In <u>Dare to Lead,</u> the amazing and eloquent Brené Brown shares her extensive research, experience, and practice on Vulnerability, Living into Our Values, Braving Trust, and Learning to Rise. If you have not read this book, I highly recommend it! On page 19, Brown writes, *"Daring is saying "I know I will eventually fail, and I'm still all in." I've never met a brave person who hasn't known disappointment, failure, and even heartbreak."* Truer words have never been spoken! She goes on to share a simple [yet life-changing] practice: **Permissions.** She used this context with her team, where each member publicly gives themselves permission [for what they need] at the onset of a team meeting. Professionally, I have used this with my Leadership Team, and the responses were amazing. I learn so much about each of us when we give ourselves permission for exactly what we need at that moment. Personally, I have adopted Permissions as well. *Today, I give myself permission not to be ok. I give myself permission to be vulnerable with others. I give myself permission not to have everything figured out. I give myself* *permission to unplug and do things that make me happy. I give myself permission to chase my wildest dreams. I give myself permission to love again.*

Consider areas of your life where you may have placed limitations or restrictions on yourself. *What specific permissions or allowances do you need to grant yourself to break free from those limitations? How can giving yourself permission contribute to your personal growth and happiness?*

Write down three permissions that you are granting yourself moving forward. *Think about how these permissions align with your values and aspirations and how they will empower you to live a more authentic and fulfilling life.*

3. Gratitude Checks

I pride myself on having a grateful heart, but a growth area of mine is verbalizing my gratitude toward others. Showing gratitude comes most naturally to me by email or text [I do that all the time], but I struggle with finding the words, looking someone in the eye, and sharing my heart. There's that fear of vulnerability again! But I am working on it. At work, I am ending meetings with Gratitude Checks and the responses have been profound! In addition, I am actively using *'Gratitude Checks'* in my daily life to capture what I am most grateful for. While these change daily, these statements show exactly who and what positively impacted my life on a given day. I've noticed that when I take the time to write down my Gratitude Checks, I am more likely to share them with the person I am grateful for. It's a Win-Win. Reader, this is so simple to do and really puts things into perspective. Things are never as good or as bad as they seem, but each one of us has something we are grateful for daily! In fact, once you begin writing down what you are grateful for, it's easy to write down a lot of things! *Currently, I am grateful for good health and personal growth. I am grateful for my mother, my biggest fan. I am grateful to everyone who believes in me. I am grateful for the immense love I feel when I look at my growing children. I am grateful for my life's work. I am grateful for the people who push me, even when I don't want to push myself. I am grateful for being loved, even when I am unlovable.*

Date:

Start a gratitude journal and write down three things you are grateful for each day for the next week. *Reflect on how this daily practice can impact your overall mood, mindset, and perspective on life.*

Now, Think about a recent challenging situation you faced and how you can reframe that experience to find something to be grateful for within it. **Write down the lessons or opportunities for growth which emerged from that situation.**

4. Surround Yourself with the Right People

I mentioned having a very small inner circle. While this is true, I have found it amazing to surround myself with individuals who provide me with tips, tools, and mentorship as I walk through my current season. I once thought that surrounding myself with like-minded people was fundamental – but my thought process has changed. While like-minded people are needed in matters of morals, core values, and beliefs, you also need people in your corner who can challenge you and push you to new heights. I now know that I need more of those people in my life. Reader, where is your journey taking you? Where are you headed? What kind of people do you need to help you accomplish it? For example, as I chase my wildest dreams, I know the kind of people I need surrounding me. *I need people who are pure of heart to offer unconditional love – the kind I feel from my family. I need people who will tell me how it is, even when it's brutal feedback. I need people who will celebrate me like I celebrate others. I need people who will be my cheerleaders and remind me to keep going, even during moments I want to give up. I need people who will make me laugh until my belly hurts. I need people who will help me keep my ego in check. I need people who will make me better, personally and professionally. I need people I can be myself around. I need people who are going to show up for me wholeheartedly, not because they have to, but because they want to.* I once thought that the people in my inner circle could be all of the things I need, but as I grow and soul-search, I believe that one person cannot be all of these things. Accepting that different people serve different purposes in my life has helped me by surrounding myself with the right people, at the precise moment. This is another opportunity to be vulnerable – seeking out the right people when you need them.

Surround Yourself with the Right People

Evaluate your current social circle or support network. *Are there any individuals who drain your energy or hurt your well-being? Consider how can you distance yourself from toxic relationships and surround yourself with more positive, supportive, uplifting people.*

Write three qualities or characteristics you value in the people you want to surround yourself with. *Think about how you can actively seek out and cultivate relationships with individuals who embody those qualities and what steps you can take to expand your network of like-minded individuals.*

----

5. Prayer and Devotionals

Last but certainly not least, as I move toward being the best version of myself and rebuilding my life, daily prayer and reading devotionals have helped me ground myself spiritually. Like most things in my life where I advocate for myself or ask for something I want or need, prayer has sometimes felt selfish, although I don't quite know why. I am working on giving myself permission to pray for exactly what I want and need. I take time and care to pray when I need it most, not only at bedtime like we teach children to do. I find comfort in morning, a mid-day, or a night-time prayer. *I pray for the big, the small, and everything in between. I pray for forgiveness. I pray for the future. I pray for my heart that is on the mend. I pray for the three people I love most. I pray for my well-being and that I am always able to care for my family. I pray for a love that keeps me smiling from the inside out. I pray for an experience that expands beyond my professional life. I pray for the best years of my life.*

These five practices have helped me turn a once painful truth into an opportunity to change my mindset and perspective. They are active processes that help me continue to grow mentally, spiritually, and emotionally. How do you turn your frown upside down? How have you learned from your own loss? How do you move forward, never forgetting the past but growing from it? I know one thing – the choice is ours.

Prayer and Devotionalse

Reflect on your spiritual or faith-based practices. *Think about how prayer and devotionals contribute to your well-being and sense of purpose. How can you deepen your connection to your spirituality or faith moving forward?*

Describe the elements or activities you would incorporate into a personal prayer or devotional practice that aligns with your beliefs and values. *Envision this practice enriching your daily life and helping you manifest your desires.*

A Final Note

Like love, loss is a natural part of this thing called life. In this process, I felt like I lost it all. I lost myself and the things I once admired. I lost the family I worked to build. I even lost the man I chose to spend my life with. I lost some of my little girl dreams. There were moments I felt like I lost myself professionally. I lost the ideation of what leadership looks like. I lost some of my passion. But please don't feel sorry for me – because oh, the things I have gained. What I have learned in this journey surpasses my loss. I have gained perspective, purpose, and belief in myself. I have gained better relationships with my children and stronger bonds are evident within our family. I have gained understanding and learned acceptance. I have gained strength and grown in faith. I have gained higher levels of self-esteem and have learned to value myself in the most authentic way. I have learned how to forgive and move past hurt. I have learned to take responsibility for my role in things and use life lessons to anchor my future decisions. I have learned to offer and extend grace. I have learned to embrace the journey and not focus so heavily on the destination. To grow, I learned to let go and stop mourning the beautiful moments of the past. Both on the home and on the work front, those moments are keepsakes of the past and shall remain tucked in my heart forever. And last but certainly not least, I have learned the power of sharing a heartfelt story to heal, to grow, and inspire. Do you remember when I was scared and uncertain? Now, I firmly believe the words of this quote, *"A ship is safe in harbor, but that's not what ships are for."* Here's to sailing toward your desired destination, despite troubled waters or uncertainty of how you will navigate challenging times. I am hopeful for my next chapter and destination! And now, I retire my pen for those who need it most – people like me who have so much to say and so much to share. Whether it's loss, joy, or trying to process something new, always remember to bet on yourself! One day, I will find my person and document my journey in the purest form. The last two years of my life have been about *Leading Through Loss* – the next phase of my life might be about *Leading in Love,* my journey to find balance, and never making the same mistakes twice. Here's to those beautiful moments that lie ahead. Here's to being unapologetically me. Here's to changing the narrative. But above all, here's to focusing less on Loss and more on the thing we call Love.

About Author

Priscilla Mendez, a seasoned educator and inspirational leader, is the accomplished Principal of an elementary school in Orlando, Florida. With seven (7) years of experience in instructional leadership, Priscilla has made a significant impact on the lives of students, teachers, and the school community.

Beyond her role as a school Principal, Priscilla extends her expertise as a respected faculty member at a local University, where she imparts her knowledge and passion through engaging lectures.

Priscilla's journey through life has been marked by both profound challenges and remarkable achievements. She has faced severities and extremities, both personally and professionally, and has emerged with an unwavering attitude of gratitude and resilience. In the face of tests, trials, and fears, Priscilla has harnessed the power of positivity to navigate through adversity and come out stronger.

Through her book, Priscilla Mendez courageously shares her personal story, aiming to inspire healing and empower readers to overcome their own pain and hardships. She believes that within each individual lies the potential for a triumph greater than any suffering endured. Priscilla invites readers to embrace a commitment to joy, irrespective of life's offerings, and to discover the transformative power of resilience.

With her wealth of experience and her ability to cultivate an uplifting mindset, Priscilla Mendez serves as a beacon of hope, guiding others toward a brighter and more fulfilling future.

PRISCILLA MENDEZ

Your Notes

Your Notes

Your Notes

Your Notes

Your Notes

Made in the USA
Monee, IL
03 October 2025

31406797R00108